Contents

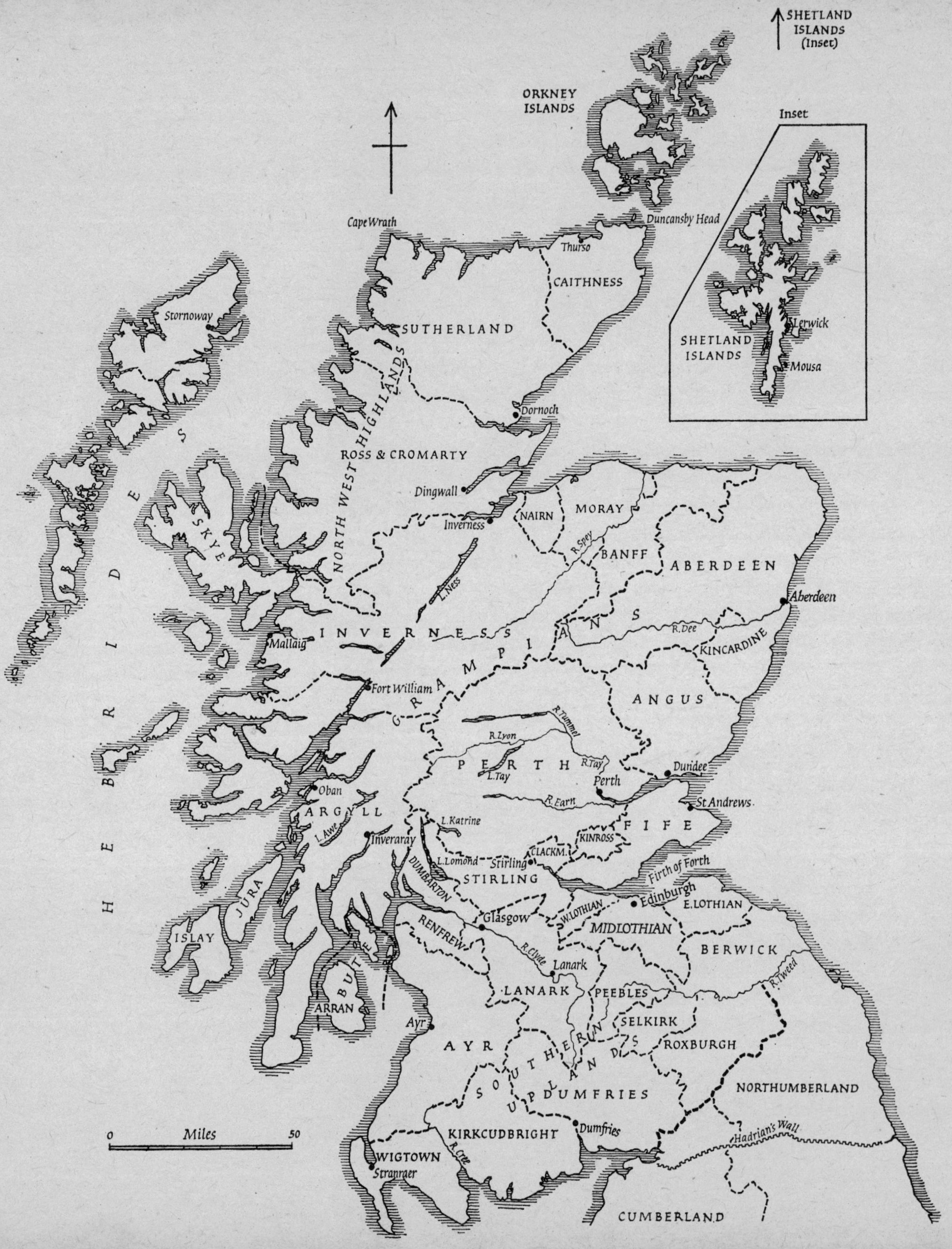

SHETLAND ISLANDS (Inset)
ORKNEY ISLANDS
Inset
Cape Wrath
Duncansby Head
Thurso
CAITHNESS
Stornoway
SUTHERLAND
SHETLAND ISLANDS
Lerwick
Mousa
NORTH WEST HIGHLANDS
Dornoch
ROSS & CROMARTY
Dingwall
Inverness
NAIRN
MORAY
R. Spey
BANFF
ABERDEEN
Aberdeen
SKYE
L. Ness
HEBRIDES
INVERNESS
GRAMPIANS
R. Dee
KINCARDINE
Mallaig
Fort William
ANGUS
R. Tummel
R. Lyon
PERTH
R. Tay
L. Tay
Dundee
Perth
Oban
R. Earn
St Andrews
ARGYLL
L. Katrine
FIFE
L. Awe
Inveraray
KINROSS
CLACKM.
L. Lomond
Stirling
DUMBARTON
Firth of Forth
STIRLING
JURA
W. LOTHIAN
Edinburgh
E. LOTHIAN
Glasgow
MIDLOTHIAN
ISLAY
RENFREW
BERWICK
R. Clyde
BUTE
Lanark
R. Tweed
LANARK
PEEBLES
ARRAN
Ayr
SELKIRK
SOUTHERN UPLANDS
ROXBURGH
AYR
DUMFRIES
NORTHUMBERLAND
0 Miles 50
KIRKCUDBRIGHT
Dumfries
Hadrian's Wall
WIGTOWN
R. Cree
Stranraer
CUMBERLAND

Scotland explored

SCOTLAND
explored

GEORGE SORLEY WHITTET

THAMES AND HUDSON · LONDON

Illustrations printed in Austria by
Christoph Reisser's Söhne AG, Vienna
Text printed in Great Britain by
Richard Clay (The Chaucer Press) Ltd, Bungay, Suffolk
500 24065 5

Historical background

From primeval times Scotland has been a place of comings and goings. The first inhabitants came from northern England and Ireland, and were for the most part hunters and fishers. Later, in about 3000 BC, people from southern Britain and the European mainland came to Scotland, bringing with them farming skills. Their presence is marked by chambered tombs, over 500 of which have been found between Galloway and Shetland.

About the middle of the first millennium BC the Celts began to arrive in Scotland. Traces of their settlements and camps, some of which were surrounded by stone walls, remain, as at the south-eastern sites of Traprain Law and the Eildon Hill.

The Romans drove into Scotland. But their attempts to bring the Celtic tribes, in particular the Picts, under their sway were not successful. The Romans built two walls to contain the marauding native bands. The first, Hadrian's Wall, stretched from the Tyne to the Solway. Their second barrier, the Antonine Wall, of which parts survive, spanned the waist of Scotland from the River Forth in the east to the River Clyde in the west.

Scotland was not known by that name until after the sixth century AD, when the Romans had returned to defend their home city and the Gaelic tribe called the Scots arrived from northern Ireland. Most famous of these was St Columba, who landed in Iona in AD 563 and established his mission of Celtic Christianity in the heathen land.

Apart from the Romans, until the arrival of the seaborne Norsemen all previous immigrations to Scotland had been relatively peaceful. The Norse descended south on the whole of Britain, Ireland and on mainland Europe, to pillage, destroy and, latterly, to settle.

When the Picts were almost wiped out by the Norsemen, Kenneth Mac Alpin, a Gaelic leader, seized the opportunity to fill the vacuum left by their defeats. He took over the land north of the Forth and became, in effect, Scotland's first 'king'.

The Norman Conquest, as such, from 1066 was the conquest of England. William of Normandy took no military action north of the Tweed. But some of the defeated English fled to Scotland, including an Anglo-Saxon princess, Margaret, who married the Scottish king Malcolm III. This lovely woman reformed the isolated Scottish church, bringing it into the broad stream of European Christianity.

The Normans coveted the fat lands of Scotland and gradually, by setting up monasteries, abbeys, cathedrals and baronial castles under the patronage of David I, who encouraged this infiltration, they became Scotland's rulers.

With the death of Alexander III in 1286 leaving no direct heir apparent, Scotland was hurled into civil conflict by contending nobles. The period that followed became historic for the War of Independence against the English Crown. Its crucial battle occurred in 1314 at Bannockburn, when Robert the Bruce soundly defeated the forces of Edward II.

In its newly established nationhood, Scotland kept pace with European emancipation. Universities were founded: St Andrews in 1412, Glasgow in 1451 and Aberdeen in 1495. Burghs grew in number under the Stuarts, the dynasty to whom the Crown passed after the death of Bruce's son, David.

Then at Flodden in 1513, James IV led the Scottish army, with the cream of the nobility, against the English troops. James was killed and Scotland suffered its greatest defeat, brought about by James' adherence to the Auld Alliance with France against England.

James V was eighteen months old when he succeeded to the throne on 21 September 1513. He, too, allied with France against England, but with no success. He died soon after hearing of his forces' defeat at Solway Moss and of the birth of his daughter, an ill-starred beauty who was to become Mary Queen of Scots.

The fate of Mary, beheaded after years of imprisonment in England, seemed almost preordained, so filled with trouble was her life. Her son, James VI of Scotland, was James I of England. With the union of the Crowns in 1603, Scotland's history as an independent country seemed almost at an end.

Almost, but not quite. When the Civil War broke out in England in 1642 between the Royalists and the Parliamentarians, Scotland fought on the side of the latter. But when Cromwell beheaded Charles I in 1649 the Scots proclaimed his son king as Charles II.

The inevitable war resulted. Cromwell triumphed and Charles fled until 1660, when he returned on the restoration of the monarchy. When Charles died in 1685 he was succeeded by his brother James VII of Scotland (James II of England). A Catholic in a primarily Protestant country, James issued a Declaration of Indulgence, giving freedom to Catholics and non-Catholics alike.

James was exceedingly unpopular in England, and English support was given to William, Prince of Orange, who was married to Mary, daughter of James. In November 1688 William landed at Torbay with an army. James VII fled to Ireland with his young son, also James, who was to become known as the 'Old Pretender' and was father of Charles Edward Stuart, 'Bonnie Prince Charlie'. In 1689 William and Mary were proclaimed king and queen of Great Britain and Ireland. There were, however, those who gave support to the exiled king, and they were known as 'Jacobites'. In 1707 the Treaty of Union was signed between the parliaments of England and Scotland. England, by Scotland's free choice, gained a dominance she could not have achieved by arms alone. The Jacobites, however, never recognized the Union, despite the fact that Scotland gained certain advantages, including free trade with England. The Jacobites were primarily concerned with unseating the Hanoverians and returning the succession to the Stuarts. (The Act of Settlement in 1701 had excluded Roman Catholics from the throne, and the right to the Crown was secured for Anne, second daughter of James II. On her death, the succession was to go to the Protestant house of Hanover.)

Two Jacobite attempts in 1715 and 1745 failed to replace the male Stuarts on the throne. The first rebellion caved in ignominiously, the second ended gallantly but sadly on Culloden Moor, when Prince Charles Edward Stuart, the Young Pretender, was brutally defeated.

The Jacobite rebellions split the Highland clans. The Campbells, for example, were pro-William III and the MacDonalds were Jacobites. This conflict had already been reflected in the massacre at Glencoe. After the 1745 rebellion, the clans were disarmed, and the chiefs were replaced by landowners, whose prime interests were in land and wealth rather than clan loyalties. Ultimately, this led to the Clearances of the eighteenth and nineteenth centuries, when poor crofters or smallholders were evicted in their hundreds by the landowners and compelled to emigrate or starve.

The Industrial Revolution transformed the Lowlands. Coal and shale mining have left unsightly refuse heaps against the horizons. The mines, steelworks, factory buildings and shipyards form the environment of more than half of Scotland's population, concentrated in a narrow Lowland strip.

Scotland has had a turbulent history. Monuments and plaques tell part of the story, but much of it can be felt only on the ground itself – in Glencoe, for example, scene of the massacre, or on the battlefield of Culloden Moor, where a cause already lost was buried.

Iona

Geography

One of the major geographical features of Scotland is the narrow waist which forms a flat band of country, defined in the north by a line running from Bowling on the lower Clyde across to Stonehaven in Kincardineshire. In the south, an almost parallel diagonal escarpment begins near Girvan in Ayrshire and ends near Dunbar in East Lothian. In this waist, the Lowlands, are the bulk of Scotland's minerals, farmland and industry, and the major seats of learning. Another band of low-lying country runs along the east coast, through the counties of Aberdeen, Banff, Moray and Nairn, as well as the tip of Caithness.

In the west and north, the Highlands and islands, the landscape swells majestically. The mountains fill the horizon. As we move on towards the sea, the land becomes flatter, and more distant horizons, where sky meets water, are visible. In much of the Highland landscape, water is trapped between massive ranges as the inland lochs ebb and flow in narrow inlets far from the open sea. Open beaches on the shores of the Moray and Dornoch Firths have broad acres of light sand.

The descriptive titles 'Highlands' and 'Lowlands' are deceptive generalizations, for there are physical features which are shared by both. The Outer Hebrides, for instance, are mostly flat and treeless islands. The Inner Hebrides, particularly the islands of Skye, Jura and Mull, are not dissimilar to the high mainland masses which they adjoin. The distinction between the Highlands and the Lowlands is based on language and tradition. In medieval Scotland, the Highlands were 'tribal' – that is, divided among the powerful clans – and were Gaelic-speaking. The feudal Lowlands were Lallans (Scots) speaking and generally did not identify with their 'barbaric' northern neighbours.

Between the Lowlands and the English border lie the Southern Uplands, which present a less spectacular landscape than the Highlands, and are sometimes classified, in defiance of geography, as part of the Lowlands.

The castle of the Earls of Seaforth at Eilean Donan –
an impressive building in a romantic landscape

Sutherland ponies

The piper. In this wind instrument the pressure is maintained by a bag made from the whole skin of a sheep or goat. It has been known in rural communities as far east as India since the 13th century. The Highland bagpipe is now the most widely used. In the past two hundred years a vast repertoire of Scottish bagpipe music has been established, and it is used for the accompanying melodies to country dances–reels, jigs and strathspeys–as well as laments and marches. A pibroch is a rousing call to arms and one of the best known is the 'Pibroch of Donuil Dhu' which may be heard today in the glens, at gatherings or played by regimental pipers on the march.

In 1816 Sir Walter Scott wrote verses in English from the Gaelic words of the old song:

Pibroch of Donuil Dhu,
Pibroch of Donuil,
Make thy wild voice anew,
Summon Clan Conuil.
Come away, come away,
Hark to the summons!
Come in your war array,
Gentles and commons.

Come from the deep glen and
From mountains so rocky,
The war-pipe and pennant
Are at Inverlochy.
Come every hill-plaid and
True heart that wears one,
Come every steel blade and
Strong hand that bears one.

From the Borders to the Firth of Clyde

Of the highroads that lead from England to Scotland, the best for a favoured view of the country is one which crosses the border at Carter Bar on the watershed of the Cheviot Hills. Most of the border-country uplands are visible, their green crests or the spinneys crowning them making individual landmarks.

Descending to the Tweed valley, one comes to Jedburgh. In this town is the first of several Augustinian abbeys which are scattered throughout Scotland. They date from their establishment in the twelfth century by a mother house at Beauvais, Saint-Quentin. Jedburgh Abbey was founded by David I, but was originally a priory. On the slowly flowing, salmon-filled River Tweed is Kelso, one of the fairest border towns. Its Tironsian abbey ruin is of a twelfth-century building; the unique Romanesque style of its west end is one of the best examples of medieval architecture in Britain.

The Tweed soon leaves Scotland and crosses the border on the east. But its upstream course leads to places of greater interest. Dryburgh Abbey, another twelfth-century ruin, lies in a quiet setting among trees by a bend in the river. Besides being an ancient monument, its significance is augmented by the tombs of two famous Scotsmen of modern times, Sir Walter Scott and Earl Haig.

The next Border Abbey, which was Cistercian, is at Melrose. It was also founded by David I, and was dedicated in 1146. It has claim to historical notice of more recent date, for here the heart of King Robert the Bruce is reputed to be buried. The carved interiors and fifteenth-century sculpture are particularly fine. Unfortunately, this and other abbeys have been used as convenient quarries for ready-shaped building stones to construct nearby secular buildings; this rather than any zealous Protestant destructiveness has reduced them to their present skeletal condition.

Sir Walter Scott, the great Romantic novelist, helped to preserve these abbeys, particularly Melrose. He lived not far distant, beside the Tweed at

Queen Mary's House, Jedburgh

◁ *Yellow gorse forms the foreground of this view of Skye*

Abbotsford in a handsome nineteenth-century mansion. His library of almost 20,000 books is still housed there.

To the west of Melrose, the countryside rises and the moors are almost empty of buildings – either secular or religious. Here we find Ettrick Forest from which many ballads have come, including the lament for Flodden, *Flowers of the Forest*. Beyond, the beautiful Yarrow valley leads to St Mary's Loch, about which Wordsworth wrote in *Yarrow Revisited*. Farther west, by Moffat, in the moors near the Devil's Beef Tub, a steep hill basin, the sources of the rivers Clyde and Tweed, best-known of all Scotland's rivers, are not more than a few miles apart.

Almost directly south of Moffat is Dumfries, an historic town that figured in the War of Independence. In later years it was the home of Robert Burns, Scotland's immortal poet. Here he worked as an exciseman. The house where he died, on 21 July 1796, remains as a monument.

Near Dumfries is the first of the great Border castles, the triangular keep of Caerlaverock, first built in the thirteenth century and besieged and captured by the English more than once. In 1583 it was rebuilt by Lord Maxwell, but in the seventeenth century suffered further when the Covenanters laid siege for thirteen weeks. Across the River Nith from Caerlaverock stands Sweetheart Abbey, the best preserved and last built Cistercian abbey in Scotland. Founded in 1275, its name derives from the fact that the foundress, Devorgilla, Lady of Galloway, lies buried in front of the High Altar with the embalmed heart of her husband, John de Baliol. He and his wife founded Balliol College, Oxford.

Dundrennan Abbey, also Cistercian and founded more than 130 years before Sweetheart, is located to the south-west of Dumfries, not far from the Solway Firth. It was here that Mary Queen of Scots may have spent her last night before she went into exile in England. The abbey is mostly in ruins, except for the transepts and the north and south walls of the choir.

If we follow the curve of Wigtown Bay we shall find the commanding Cardoness Castle overlooking the inlet, a fifteenth-century tower house. Not far away is Green Tower Motte, an example of the crude enclosures that were the first Norman 'castles' in Scotland.

Arran

On the far shore is Whithorn, among the most significant Christian localities in all Scotland. Here St Ninian built a stone church in AD 397, the earliest in the country, when the Saint's mission began. His shrine is in the church which was built in the thirteenth century on the remains of a twelfth-century structure. Under the ruins lie the foundations of St Ninian's original little chapel.

The last abbey in Galloway is Glenluce, a twelfth-century Cistercian

Loch Trool and the Bruce Memorial ▷

Above: ivy climbs a wall at Dryburgh Abbey, founded 1150
Left: Jedburgh Abbey, founded 1118. Even in their ruins the Scottish abbeys radiate a great peace. Like the Acropolis in Athens, the Forum in Rome and the tall trees of the forest, time adds to their aura

Bare, ruined choirs: the ruins of Jedburgh Abbey (left) and Sweetheart Abbey (right). Sweetheart Abbey owes its name to the fact that its founder, Lady Devorgilla, lies buried beside the heart of her husband in front of the high altar

Melrose Abbey, founded in 1136, was restored after many of its stones had been removed for building. Sir Walter Scott, who lived nearby, did much to preserve the Border Abbeys

Culzean Castle, built in 1777–92, with its beautifully laid-out gardens in which palm trees grow, is one of the most imposing castles in the south of Scotland

Below: Abbotsford, home of the great Scottish novelist Sir Walter Scott (1771–1832)

Right: The Burns Memorial at Alloway. Robert Burns (1759–1796), Scotland's national poet and one of the world's greatest, wrote a poem that could be his own epitaph:

Is there a man whose judgment clear,
Can others teach the way to steer,
Yet runs himself life's mad career,
Wild as the wave?
Here let him pause, and through a tear
Survey this grave.

The Globe Inn, Dumfries, a favourite tavern of Robert Burns

foundation of which little remains. But the fine fifteenth-century chapter house is almost intact.

Galloway is also rich in natural beauty. To the north is Glen Trool National Forest Park, covering 203 square miles. This luxuriant region encompasses many lochs, valleys and mountains, including Loch Trool, and the Merrick, with its five peaks, which rises to 2,764 feet. To the west is the sea and the coast road leading towards Ayr. Ten miles from the shore is the volcanic rock Ailsa Craig, whose sole occupants are a lighthouse and multitudes of sea birds.

There are more than one thousand castles in Scotland, in varying states of repair. The preponderance of such structures has, in fact, influenced more modern architecture. Culzean Castle, built in 1777–92 for the Marquis of Ailsa by the brilliant eighteenth-century architect Robert Adam, has medieval trimmings typical of the Picturesque Style. Adam, who studied in Italy, wrote a book recommending many improvements to Edinburgh. That city is indebted to him for many of its finest buildings, including the Register House and Charlotte Square.

Ayr is an old town, although little of its original structure is left. For many Scots, Ayr is noteworthy not for its antiquity, but because Robert Burns went to school there. He was born on the outskirts, at Alloway. A museum is now attached to the cottage where he was born, which houses many of his original manuscripts as well as his private possessions.

The Ayrshire coast forms one shore of the Firth of Clyde. Its ports, Ardrossan and Ayr, give access to the islands of the Clyde. These are essentially both Hebridean and Highland, even though they are farther south than Edinburgh.

Arran is the largest of these islands. In its northern half the mountains rise steeply from sea level, so that Goatfell, 2,866 feet high, seems to loom larger than a higher peak on the mainland. From the summit cairn, the view on all sides reveals Scotland's diversity – the sea and the islands, the lowland valleys and the bens of the north. From Brodick Castle, set in the dark green of the trees, Robert the Bruce launched his long campaign against the English that led to victory at Bannockburn in 1314. The Castle, once the seat of the Dukes of Hamilton, is surrounded by magnificent gardens.

North of Arran is the island of Bute, where in summer crowded little steamboats carry travellers from Glasgow for a day at Rothesay. In idyllic seclusion, one can smell the aromatic scent of the Highlands and see some of their beauty across the Argyll narrows, known as the Kyles of Bute.

Edinburgh and the Lothians

Of all Scottish cities, Edinburgh holds pride of place. It is, of course, the capital of Scotland, a position it took in 1452, when James II held his parliament there. But Edinburgh's unique identity is based on the less obvious distinction of having an intangible but psychologically powerful division from England.

Edinburgh, like Rome, is built on seven hills. The highest place is the Castle Rock, where David II built a fortress tower more than 600 years ago. Its passages and chambers honeycomb the rock itself. Edward I of England captured the Castle in 1296, but the Earl of Moray, in 1314, took it for Robert the Bruce, who swore the English would never again occupy it. From 1337 to 1341, Edward III of England held it. Cromwell captured it in 1650, after the Battle of Dunbar.

St Margaret's Chapel is the oldest building in Edinburgh. It was built by Malcolm III's queen, Margaret, who heard Mass here before she died in 1093. Intimate and simple, it holds fewer than thirty worshippers.

In the south-east corner of Crown Square is a tiny room of the palace, part of Queen Mary's apartments, where Mary gave birth to a son who was to become James VI of Scotland and James I of England. Also in the old palace is the Crown Room, which contains the ancient Regalia of the Scottish kings, which was hidden for more than 100 years after the Union of the Parliaments in 1707.

From the Castle, with its marvellous vista across the eastern lowlands to the bens of Perthshire in the north-west, the Esplanade opens into the Lawnmarket. This street commences the 'Royal Mile' which ends at the Palace of Holyrood. It goes through the Old Town of Edinburgh, like a spine of venerable buildings. Here is Gladstone's Land, a richly decorated seventeenth-century town house that is well preserved. Other places along the Royal Mile include Lady Stair's Close and Lady Stair's House, as well as Brodie's Close.

Dunfermline Abbey

View of Edinburgh

Walking through Edinburgh.
Left: Old Dean Bridge
Right: The Scott Monument in Princes Street

WAVERLEY HOTEL

Left: Edinburgh Castle, high above the city. Below: John Knox's House, former home of the Scottish Reformer, is one of the oldest in Edinburgh

The famous Forth Bridges. The old bridge was built in 1883–90, the new road bridge in 1958–64. More than one and a half miles long, it soars more than 300 feet above the waters of the Firth of Forth

The Bass Rock. This natural pillar of stone, which stands at the entrance to the Firth of Forth, is seen beyond the ruins of Tantallon Castle, built in the 14th century

Left: the Prentice Pillar in Roslin Chapel. According to the legend this stone carving was executed by an apprentice unknown to his master who, discovering the truth, killed him from sheer envy

Right: Hopetoun House, built in the 18th century

Edinburgh: the entrance gates of Holyroodhouse

In the garden of Hopetoun House

Linlithgow Palace, birth-place of Mary Queen of Scots in 1542

Gifford, at the foot of the Lammermuir Hills. Time does not stand still here but passes more quietly

Holyroodhouse, Edinburgh

Farther on, the Lawnmarket becomes High Street and we come upon the High Kirk of St Giles, dating from before the Reformation. Although it is sometimes called a cathedral, it has only briefly been such. It is surmounted by the noblest remaining fragment of its original architecture, a Gothic lantern spire (the 'Crown'), completed about 1495. Much restoration has left little else intact of the twelfth-century design.

In nearby Parliament Square is Parliament House, a nineteenth-century façade erected on the site of the previous Gothic building, redundant since 1707 as a parliament but now housing the Court of Session, supreme court of Scotland. In the Square is the grave of John Knox, famous sixteenth-century Calvinist preacher and foe of Catholic Queen Mary. At the lower end of High Street stands his house, which is preserved as a memorial.

Now High Street becomes Canongate, as it approaches the gates of Holyroodhouse. Here are many of the grand town houses which belonged to the nobility. One of them, Huntly House, is today a rambling, but impressive, museum.

The Palace of Holyroodhouse, at the end of the Royal Mile, stands under the height of Arthur's Seat, a spur of the Pentland Hills. The Palace was begun in 1500 by James IV, but a fire in 1544 destroyed nearly all of it. Beyond the courtyard is the Chapel Royal, which alone remains of Holyrood Abbey. The Abbey was founded in 1128 by David I, and it was here that the miraculous agency of the Holy Cross is said to have saved him. It is from this legend that the name Holyrood derives.

After the Union the Palace remained largely unused until Queen Victoria restored it. But its apartments seem filled with the sad memories of its occupants of four centuries ago. For it was here that David Rizzio, Queen Mary's ill-fated Italian secretary, was murdered.

Across the North Bridge, which spans the built-up valley of a former marshland, one enters the New Town of Edinburgh, begun as part of the city's expansion in 1767. To the north of gracious Princes Street, this part of Edinburgh has a spacious neo-classic character, which derives primarily from the energies of an early town planner, James Craig. Fortunately, the time for such civic improvement was ripe, for in 1752, a pamphlet called *Proposals for carrying on certain public works in the city of Edinburgh* was published, in which it was stated that 'At no period surely did there ever appear a more general, or a better directed zeal for the improvement and prosperity of the country.' So it was with such spirit that the decision to build a new Edinburgh was made. A nationwide competition for the layout of the New Town was won by young James Craig.

Scotland is well known for standing by its failures no less than by its successes. Near to the Register House, a handsomely proportioned building at the east end of Princes Street designed by Robert Adam, is Calton Hill. On its summit is all that was ever constructed of a copy of the Parthenon which was to be erected as a memorial to the Scots who fell in the Napoleonic wars. Twelve columns were raised, then the money was exhausted. The architect concerned, W. H. Playfair, fared better with his designs for the two classically impressive buildings midway along Princes Street, the National Gallery of Scotland, home of many masterpieces, and the Royal Scottish Academy.

This happy contrast between the medieval and the classic so evident in Edinburgh is present elsewhere in the Lothians, the counties which surround the city. But Edinburgh has its share of modern architecture and engineering too, exemplified by the steel and concrete structures of the Forth Bridges.

Near the southern approach to the new Forth Road Bridge is Hopetoun House, the stately home of the Marquis of Linlithgow. Set in open parkland with gardens modelled on the plan of Versailles, the long curving front is the joint triumph of four architects: Sir William Bruce, who designed the central building, William Adam his pupil and the latter's sons Robert and John. Completed in 1752, Hopetoun House remains unaltered as a masterpiece of Scotland's greatest period of architecture.

Not far to the west beside Linlithgow Loch is the still impressive stone ruin of Linlithgow Palace, begun by James I in 1425. A later Stuart king, James V, was to bring his bride, Mary of Guise, here, where she gave birth to a daughter who was to become Mary Queen of Scots.

In the Lothians are the ruins of several medieval towers, most of them roofless. Some, by chance rather than intention, have been well preserved. One of these is Borthwick Castle, situated on the road to Galashiels from Edinburgh. It is a four-square block of faced stone walls 110 feet high and of unusual thickness. Built in 1430 by Lord Borthwick, it is still occupied by the Borthwick family. It was besieged only once, when Cromwell's guns required but a single fusillade to produce its surrender.

East of Edinburgh we come to Haddington, a quiet town on the route from Berwick-upon-Tweed. Today its appearance is a distinguished one, for it has many fine seventeenth- and eighteenth-century buildings, some of which were designed by Robert Adam. To the north of Haddington lies Tantallon Castle, a grand fourteenth-century fortress of the powerful Douglas family; spanning a headland almost impregnably, it provides a man-made complement to the natural pillar of the Bass Rock, which rises 350 feet from the waters of the Firth of Forth below the castle.

The lush Lothians abound in flashing views of the Forth from the hills and, from their upper heights in the Pentlands, of the quiet valleys. Sequestered in this rural environment, one finds almost concealed villages which have an historic atmosphere and individual character. Gifford and East Linton, both close to Haddington, are typical of these little towns. Concealed, too, are such architectural gems as the chapel of Roslin Castle, only seven miles from Edinburgh. In 1446, Sir William Sinclair began the collegiate church of which this is the choir. The carved stone decoration is unique and is possibly the work of a Spanish craftsman.

Glasgow and the Lowlands

Although Glasgow's immediate impact is that of a highly industrialized modern city and a thriving commercial seaport, it has even more ancient origins than Edinburgh. The diocese of Glasgow was established in 1136, its university was founded in 1451. But Glasgow's thriving growth as the centre of Scotland's shipbuilding and chemical industries has meant that, unlike Edinburgh, its earliest traces have been absorbed and obscured by the proliferation of modern building. With an ever-increasing population, it is Scotland's largest city.

In early days Glasgow was a market town of a rich agricultural community clustered round a ford of the River Clyde. It was only in the eighteenth century, when maritime trade with the Americas increased rapidly, that Glasgow really flourished. The tobacco lords built handsomely, but little has survived.

Most of the major building in Glasgow dates from the nineteenth century, when the Industrial Revolution brought greater prosperity. Victorian architecture predominates in the squares and the streets around George Square, the civic centre. One of the only extant buildings from Glasgow's early past is the twelfth-century Cathedral. In the Early Pointed style, it is one of the finest examples of Gothic ecclesiastical building in Scotland. It is particularly noted for the fan-vaulted crypt, which is lit by forty-one windows, and it is where St Mungo, the city's patron saint, is said to be buried.

The oldest house in Glasgow is known as Provand's Lordship, in the High Street. It dates from 1471, but it has little apart from its survival to interest anyone; it is now a museum of domestic furniture. Parts of older buildings remain in the Tolbooth Steeple (1626) and the Tron Steeple (1637).

The most notable 'modern' building in Glasgow is the School of Art in Renfrew Street, which was designed by Charles Rennie Mackintosh after winning a competition in 1896. This rather austere building has received wide attention for being a forerunner of the 'modern' school of architecture. The interior is equally revolutionary in conception.

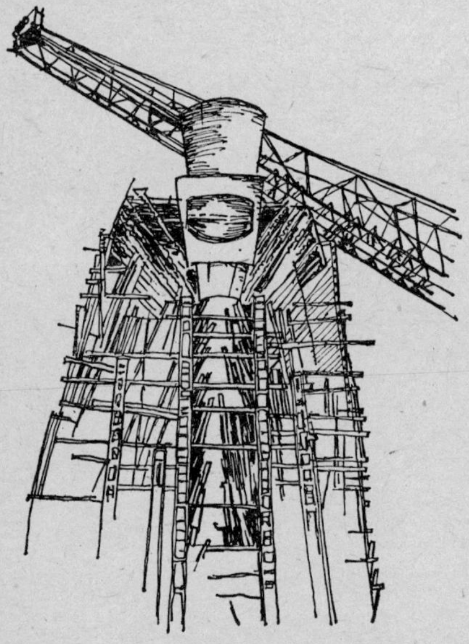

Glasgow shipyard

Glasgow, port and commercial centre

Old and modern architecture. Left: The Cathedral of Glasgow, built in the 12th century
Below: a training college for priests (founded 1966) at Cardross near Glasgow

On the following two pages: Stirling Castle, a favourite residence of the Stuart kings

Glamis Castle. Today's building dates from the 17th century, but according to tradition it was on the former site of a castle where the original tragedy of Macbeth was enacted

St Andrews Cathedral, built in the 12th century, was destroyed in 1559 after the Reformation. The dignity of this 100-yard-long building perished when its stones were removed for other buildings

St Andrews, once a focal point in Scottish history, is today a fashionable holiday resort and world-famous home of golf

Arbroath Abbey

From Gilmorehill, Glasgow University looks down on the richly endowed City Art Gallery in the pleasant park of Kelvingrove. Both the University and the Gallery are highly flamboyant examples of Victorian Gothic (the University has been called 'Scotland's first space probe').

Although most of the medieval buildings around Glasgow have not survived, Bothwell Castle, a stronghold built in the thirteenth and fifteenth centuries, is a dramatically large and substantial ruin.

Probably the most strategically placed castle in Scotland is at Stirling. It is one of the four castles which had to be kept up and garrisoned under the terms of the Act of Union (the other three being Edinburgh, Blackness and Dumbarton). Occupied as a royal palace from the fifteenth century onwards, when the Stuart monarchs regularly resided there, it stands on the high rock that dominates the town.

In the vicinity of Stirling is the scene of the most famous battle of the War of Independence: Bannockburn in 1314. Here Robert the Bruce defeated the English forces. Like so many historical battlefields, its interest relies on the knowledge of a past event rather than on the impact of its present appearance.

East of Stirling and into Fife, there is another ancient royal burgh, Dunfermline. It was at one time the seat of the Scottish court, which met in a thirteenth-century palace of which traces remain. Next to it is a substantial ruin of the abbey church of Holy Trinity, the remains of a Benedictine monastery founded by David I in 1128, on the site of Queen Margaret's church. Despite restoration and additions, the twelfth-century nave remains the finest example in Scotland of the Romanesque style. Seven Scottish kings are buried here, including Robert the Bruce.

Near to Dunfermline is Culross. Here, the foundations of the Parish Church, part of a Cistercian abbey church which was founded in 1217, remain. A small palace, built in 1597–1611, also exists. Falkland Palace, a hunting lodge of the

Stuart kings, contains some fine work by French sculptors in the preserved interior.

St Andrews, on a bay of the North Sea, is an historic centre of both religion and education. The cathedral-priory, which was founded in 1169 by Bishop Arnold, has been largely destroyed, both by natural forces and by post-Reformation builders. Only the sixteenth-century outer wall of the Augustinian priory remains, within which are the fragments of the Cathedral. The church itself was 355 feet long, with a nave which had fourteen bays, a figure exceeded by Norwich Cathedral alone. Unfortunately, only the east and west gables and parts of the nave and south transept remain of what was once the largest church in Scotland. St Rule's, the first Augustinian church in the country, with its square tower, adjoins the cathedral-priory. The elements have ravaged the old castle of St Andrew's too. Rebuilt at the end of the fourteenth century, it was destroyed again, and the sea has undermined it till only a tower and a dungeon of grim reputation remain.

To reach Angus from Fife a new road bridge spans the Tay. But it is more pleasant to take the longer way round so that a visit may be made to Perth, the so-called 'Fair City'. Its setting is certainly of the fairest, for it sits beside the broad meadows watered by the Tay.

Architecturally, Perth has only vestiges of the neo-classic style which, in Scotland, originated in Edinburgh during the late eighteenth century and kept up its momentum in other localities until well into the nineteenth. There are only a few of the more ancient buildings extant, of which the town church of St John the Baptist is one of the most beautiful.

Crossing into Angus, we are soon in the broad valleys of Strathmore, an earldom of which the family seat is Glamis Castle. This is an outstanding example of the Scottish baronial style of the late seventeenth century. It was here that Princess Margaret was born in 1930.

Dundee, at the mouth of the Tay estuary, is the chief port of this region. In the course of its troubled history, most of its notable buildings have been obliterated; on no fewer than three occasions the English pillaged and fired the city, destroying, among others, the old church of St Mary's. There remains only the Old Steeple, built in the mid-fifteenth century.

On the north Angus coast, the town of Arbroath is notable for the ruins of the Cluniac abbey, founded in 1175 by the Scottish king William 'the Lion'; his remains lie buried here. In the south transept is a fine rose window which dates from the thirteenth century. For Scots the abbey has historic associations. In 1320, the parliament, made up of nobles and church leaders, met here to draw up the Declaration of Independence, addressed to the pope.

The Highlands

Stirling has been called 'the Gateway to the Highlands'. But for most people, and certainly for Glasgow's growing population, the Highlands begin just a short distance away on Loch Lomond. Celebrated in the nostalgic song sung by Scottish exiles everywhere, its peaceful beauty is a refreshing contrast to the industrial monotony of Clydeside. Loch Lomond is the largest lake in Great Britain, twenty-four miles long, up to five miles wide and a maximum depth of over 600 feet. Its coast is often wooded and there are a number of small islands which make it a constant source of visual delight.

Many of the mountains that flank the loch come into the category of a 'Munro', a peak rising to at least 3,000 feet above sea level. Ben Lomond, on the east, is a Munro and there are several to the west above Loch Long where the road zig-zags upwards to the ridge; from there it almost plummets down to Loch Fyne. This road crest is known as the 'Rest and Be Thankful', and at one time, for the traveller on foot or on horseback, this was a truly significant phrase.

Descending to Loch Fyne's shore, the whitewashed buildings of Inveraray soon come into view. Inveraray is one of the most picturesque towns in the Highlands. Close at hand is Inveraray Castle, the ancestral home of the Duke of Argyll, hereditary chieftain of the Clan Campbell. Set on a slope above the Aray River the startling blue-green granite castle and its surroundings epitomize the Scottish romantic landscape. The castle was built in 1746, although much restoration and addition has been done since then.

The town of Inveraray is the result of an eighteenth-century plan. Designed by Robert Mylne, it is formal and remarkably austere. The houses are mostly undecorated three-storey cottages.

North from salt-water Loch Fyne lies long and narrow fresh-water Loch Awe, its islands guarding the ruins of old castles once occupied under the

Oban

At the Highland Games

Campbells. The best-known of these is Kilchurn, standing foursquare on its fifteenth-century foundations, secure in a scene of true Highland grandeur. Lofty Ben Cruachan swells over the Pass of Brander to the north-west, where the salmon-filled outflow of the loch joins Loch Etive.

Almost at Loch Etive's mouth on the breast of the sea, the road turns southerly towards Oban. This handsome, busy Victorian town is a harbour terminal for many of the steamboat services running to the Inner and Outer Hebrides. It faces the Isle of Mull, often visible only by the peaks which rise above the swirling morning mist. On Battery Hill behind Oban is the imposing amphitheatre which was going to be a combined view tower and cultural centre, but which was abandoned. An ambitious building, sponsored by a local benefactor in the late nineteenth century, it bears his name as McCaig's Tower.

If we turn north to cross into Benderloch, we find just outside Oban the renowned thirteenth-century feudal castle of Dunstaffnage, another stronghold of the Campbells with, close by, the ruined Gothic chapel.

After crossing Benderloch we enter Appin. This area, clawed by the sea into deep inlets, has also suffered historically, for here was one of the centres of Jacobite support for the lost Stuart cause. At Ballachulish the mountainside is scarred by slate quarries, and everywhere the views are awesome and stark. The storied pass of Glencoe is in this region. Here, in 1692, at the 'Glen of Weeping', the MacDonalds were attacked by men of the Earl of Argyll's Regiment, led by Campbell of Glenlyon. Although the oath of allegiance to William III had been taken by the chief, Alasdair MacDonald, his submission (which had come five days after the deadline) was brutually ignored, and the massacre was ordered. Thirty-eight people were killed, the rest fled into the mountains, where many more died.

Across the still waters of Loch Leven, the mountains of the Mamore Forest (a forest in Scotland is not necessarily of trees; it may be only a covering of scrub and heather) are the outposts to the highest mountain in Great Britain: Ben Nevis. Its rounded summit, 4,406 feet high, rises above Fort William, a vital communications link where the Caledonian Canal begins. This waterway links the lochs that run through the Great Glen, which divides Scotland from south-west to north-east.

The stories of the Rebellions of 1715 and 1745 are everywhere present in the Highlands. Particularly the story of the gallant Prince Charles Edward Stuart, the Young Pretender, who raised his father's, James VIII's, standard to the west of Fort William by lonely Loch Shiel, in August 1745. At lovely Glenfinnan at the head of the loch, the memorial to the event, built in 1815, stands like a lookout tower.

Loch Maree in Western Ross-shire ▷

Below: Loch Linnhe at Corpach. In the background is Ben Nevis, highest mountain in Scotland (4,418 ft). It was here that Keats composed his famous poem 'Written Upon the Top of Ben Nevis'

Loch Ness, a scene of peaceful beauty though it has gained a wider fame as the home of a reputed monster. Photographs exist that purport to show this mammoth sea serpent, though they are admittedly indistinct. Scientists and others have investigated, but the mystery persists

Today's traveller in Scotland may think of whiskey, bagpipes and tartans. But those who are interested in delving into the past will find that there are many events in Scottish history which are unparalleled in excitement and intrigue. The War of Independence against the English, for example, was marked by episodes of great daring and courage. Perhaps the most horrific conflict of all was between the Highland clans. In the bleak landscape of Glencoe (right), a massacre occurred which even today is unforgotten. A party of men from the Clan Campbell were given the traditional hospitality of the Highlands by the MacDonalds. However, after several days as guests, the Campbells attacked and murdered thirty-eight MacDonalds, including women and children. The monument (below) bears witness to this tragic event of 1692

Loch Rannoch. 'Mighty Scottish landscape, brooding and melancholy', was how the painter Gilpin described the beautiful scene at the end of the 18th century. He was impressed by the immensity of the mountain ranges and the force of wind and wave on both coast and inland lochs

Left: a ranch, but not in the American West. This is in Inverness-shire near Fort William, where Scottish farmers have begun to breed beef cattle in recent years with some success
Right: the Peaks of Kintail

Below: Loch Leven

Right: Near Eilean Donan in western Ross-shire

Glenfinnan. Here in a romantic setting is one more reminder of Scotland's long struggle for independence. The memorial, erected in 1815, marks the spot where Prince Charles Edward Stuart raised his father's standard in 1745

One road to the Isles leads west to Arisaig and Mallaig, but farther north is an equally exciting one by Glen Garry that reaches to Loch Aish and north again to Loch Torridon. Here the landscape is suffused with glorious red tints on the rock faces of the northern peaks.

The unique gardens at Inverewe at the head of Loch Ewe are aflame with floral colour. Exotic flowers and richly hued tropical plants present an unexpected visual joy against the mountainous backdrop. Not far distant is Loch Maree, possibly in itself and in its situation the most wonderful loch in Scotland, dotted with wooded islets and flanked by Ben Eighe, a national nature reserve. On one of Loch Maree's islands, a seventh-century saint, Maelrubhe, is said to have had his hermitage.

The grand and the bleak alternate in Sutherland, where fishing villages, typified by Lochinver, and crofting villages such as Scourie, enjoy the benefits of Gulf Stream warmth. The climatic conditions allow even palm trees to grow in sheltered gardens, though this is a latitude more than two degrees farther north than Moscow. But the bleak beauty of mountains and moorland, broken only by rivers and lochs, is almost numbing, particularly in the more uninhabited regions. At times, Scotland's grandeur seems reduced to a desolate wasteland.

To reach the heights of the Grampians, south of the Caledonian Canal, the road leads to Inverness, the 'capital' of the Highlands from prehistoric times. Unlike Glasgow and Edinburgh, the comparatively modern architecture of Inverness is undistinguished. However, it is the only sizeable town in the Highlands. It is important geographically rather than historically or architecturally, but is not without considerable charm. Standing on the River Ness, gracefully bridged, it is the departure point of a good highway that leads up to Aviemore on the breast of the Cairngorms.

The Cairngorms are a mountain range of massive proportions, with four of the highest peaks in Scotland. This region is naturally an ideal place for winter sport, and the slopes are excellent for skiing. Turning south into the centre of the Grampian mountains, the drop of the road through the narrow Pass of Killiecrankie, scene of a battle between Jacobites and William III's army, leads us to less rugged horizons.

Here the Perthshire Highlands present a more sympathetic landscape. Though the mountains rise to great heights, their rocky surfaces are often covered with vegetation, and the many lochs are lined by the warm green of trees. Loch Rannoch, Loch Tay and Loch Earn have a particular charm that is not marred by the several hydro-electric systems which are harnessed to their power.

Rebuilt in the so-called 'Scottish Baronial' style of the nineteenth century, Blair Castle at Blair Atholl is occupied by the Duke of Atholl. The original fortress dates from the latter half of the thirteenth century, but little of it survives. Having undergone a number of restorations, it is now almost entirely Victorian. Nearby towns, such as Pitlochry and Aberfeldy, Comrie and Crieff, provide hotel amenities for the tourist. This part of Scotland has been populated since antiquity, and there are at Pitlochry Pictish sculptured stones which testify to this fact. Aberfeldy has a well-constructed bridge, the last that was built by General Wade in his campaign for the pacification of the Highlands after the 1715 Rebellion. In Dunkeld are the ruins of a once splendid medieval cathedral, begun in the fourteenth century.

The Hebrides

There are more than five hundred islands which comprise the Inner and Outer Hebrides, off the west coast. From the northernmost Butt of Lewis to Barra Head in the south is a total distance of 130 miles; at their greatest breadth, the Hebrides are thirty miles wide. Because the islands are mostly rock (*archaean gneiss*, the oldest rock known), little of the land is arable, and so only about one-fifth of them are inhabited. Potatoes and turnips are the only successful root crops, and barley and oats are also grown. Many of the islanders support themselves by raising livestock, and there is some industry, including fishing and distilling. Of course, with their extraordinary bleak beauty and the wealth of ancient monuments, the Hebrides attract many tourists.

In the ninth century, Scandinavians, fleeing from the rule of the Norwegian King Harald Fairhair, settled in large numbers on the islands. These exiled peoples soon afterwards returned to attack their mother country, and finally Harald invaded and conquered. The Norwegians kept the islands until, after their defeat at Largs in 1263, Magnus concluded a peace treaty with the Scots, keeping only Orkney and Shetland as Norwegian possessions, which they remained until 1472.

Long before the Norse immigration, St Columba had left his native Ireland in 563 to settle in Iona. Among the heathen Picts, St Columba preached and won many converts, including one of their kings, Brude. There are possible traces of St Columba's original cell above the rocky outcrop Tor Abb. In the thirteenth century, a Benedictine abbey was built near this spot, which, in the fifteenth century, became the Cathedral Church. This has been greatly restored, particularly in this century, but much of the original design of the Scottish Romanesque plan is discernible.

Remnants of past civilizations are evident in the chambered cairns, earth-houses, standing stones and crosses. Among the latter are St Martin's Cross and

Whisky distillery in the Hebrides

Kildatton Cross, the only extant crosses in Scotland with their wheel-heads intact.

Nearer to the coast of Scotland proper are the Inner Hebrides, the most southerly island of which is Islay, just to the west of Kintyre, the peninsula that shelters the Firth of Clyde from the Atlantic. Islay is a fertile island, with farmland and peaty moors. As a result of regular contact with Ireland in early times, there are a number of ancient Celtic crosses to be found here, as well as the ruins of some pre-Reformation chapels.

Jura, lying close to Islay, is more craggy and, covered in moorland brown, it seems more like the Highlands. Its range of three peaks rise to 2,569 feet. Known as the Paps of Jura, the terrain, where the most common quadruped is the deer, presents a challenge to climbers.

One of the most appealing of islands is Mull, second largest of the Inner Hebrides. Tobermory is the chief township of Mull. In its bay lies the wreck of a flagship of the Spanish Armada, which fled from the English admiral Drake after the famous sea battle of almost four hundred years ago. Treasure hunters still hope to find great riches in its wreck. The island itself has little wealth, and many of its inhabitants have been forced to emigrate by wealthy landholders who wish to use the desolate land for sheep raising. High above all, the curving summit of Ben More towers. Duart Castle, almost opposite Oban at Duart Point, is the restored stronghold of the Macleans, one of the great Highland clans who once ruled Mull and its neighbouring islands.

On the Isle of Skye

One of the Celtic crosses in Islay

Iona. On this tiny island of the Inner Hebrides, St Columba landed from Ireland in 563, bringing the Christian religion to Scotland. This picture shows a sculpture by Epstein erected in the cloister of the reconstructed abbey in 1938

Left: the ruins of Duntulm Castle in Skye

Below: one of the world's smaller wonders is Fingal's Cave in the basalt island of Staffa. The entrance is over 60 feet high and in small boats visitors can enter the cave

Portree means 'the King's Port', but it is little more than a landing place in a small bay of Skye (picture below). In the harbours of the Hebrides, life is peaceful. The picture on the right shows Tobermory, chief port of the Isle of Mull

Jura, island of the Inner Hebrides

Another tiny island of chiefly geological interest lies west of Mull and is called Staffa. On this small islet are pillar-like structures of basalt which were formed by volcanic activity. These curious formations have attracted many writers, artists and musicians, Wordsworth and Mendelssohn among them. Mendelssohn's famous 'Fingal's Cave' overture was inspired by the phenomenal natural cave on the island.

To the north of Mull, closer to the mainland, is Skye. In plan a rampant dragon, it seems dynamically poised to leap from the Sound of Sleat towards the shining expanse of the Atlantic. Skye is the largest of the Western Isles and undoubtedly the most famous. From whatever direction one approaches it, the most prominent feature on the skyline is the Cuillins, the group of peaks to the south of the island that present some of the most exciting rock faces in Scotland to the experienced climber.

Like most of the Hebrides, Skye was a Norse dominion until 1263. Since then, the ruling island clan has been the Macleods of Dunvegan, whose castle is one of the most imposing buildings on the west coast. Strategically placed, its site has been the home of the clan chieftain since the thirteenth century. Man and nature compete architecturally in Skye as elsewhere in Scotland; in the north-east, a ridge of basalt peaks at Trotternish are topped by the massive toothed pinnacles known as the Quiraing and the Old Man of Storr.

The chief town and port of Skye is Portree. It has a fine natural harbour and its white-washed houses are a sparkling welcome. It was to this island that Flora MacDonald helped Prince Charles Edward Stuart escape, after the debacle of Culloden in 1746.

Opposite Portree is Raasay, a long narrow island which another branch of the clan Macleod at one time possessed. Skye and Raasay both suffered from the Clearances of the eighteenth and nineteenth centuries. In Skye, however, the crofters revolted in the 1880s. This eventually induced Gladstone, the British Prime Minister, to enact a law to protect the rights of the smallholders. Skye is still populated by many crofters, though in recent years their number has been reduced.

Today crofters still predominate in Barra, the most remote of the inhabited islands of the Outer Hebrides and southernmost in the string separated from Skye and the mainland of Ross and Cromarty by the Minches, stretches of open sea. The crofters' cottages, simple and solid, appear almost to have become part of the surrounding land.

Between Barra and Uist is the lovely island of Eriskay, the first Scottish earth on which 'Bonnie Prince Charlie' stood when he arrived from France to launch his ill-fated rebellion.

North from Eriskay is South Uist, which is probably the most typically Celtic community in the Hebrides. Lacking a central town – Lochboisdale is its port – the crofters lead isolated lives. Hilly in parts, the island has more than 190 fresh-water lochs. Its northern neighbours, Benbecula and North Uist, which are connected by a causeway, are also spotted with many of these little fresh-water reservoirs, alive with trout.

There is evidence in North Uist of ancient religions. Burial places, marked by circles of stone, monoliths and cairns with interior chambers from prehistoric times can be found. Near Carinish there is a ruined church that dates from the fourteenth century. It still retains its Gaelic name, for that language is still spoken by most of the islanders.

Lewis and Harris are not, in fact, islands, but two portions of the largest and northernmost island. Their differences, however, are evident. Lewis, the larger of the two, is rugged and rocky. Its chief town, Stornoway, is largely modern, having been planned as a port in the eighteenth century. Harris, the lower part, is famous for the tweed cloth that bears its name. Its scenery is varied: wild and verdant.

The North-east, Orkney and Shetland

Although the Highland Fault (the escarpment that more or less divides the mountains from the lesser slopes) ends north of Stonehaven, actually what are generally considered the Lowlands continue into the coastal plains of the counties of Aberdeen, Banff, Moray, Nairn, Ross and Cromarty and Caithness.

Aberdeenshire's chief rivers are easily remembered as the two D's – Dee and Don – and while each has its source in the Cairngorm Mountains, they both run broad and smooth in their quiet lower reaches. Here, amidst the green and fertile acres, the salmon fishing is excellent. Balmoral, Braemar and Ballater have the atmosphere of the Highlands. Balmoral Castle, where the Queen frequently spends part of the summer, was completed in the nineteenth century for Queen Victoria on the site of an old fortress which had already been reconstructed. It is, in effect, a royal shooting lodge on a grand scale.

Upstream on the Dee, Braemar is the popular winter sports resort, and the annual venue of the Highland Gathering where piping and field events are the main attractions. Braemar Castle, originally built in 1628, was burned down some sixty years later, rebuilt and eventually taken over by the government as a military post. Its architecture is now stylistically inconsistent, though its eight-pointed curtain wall 'star' shape is an orthodox continental eighteenth-century fortification pattern comparatively uncommon in Britain.

On the North Sea coast, at the mouth of the River Dee, is Aberdeen, the 'granite city'. Its main thoroughfare, Union Street, is largely built in the neo-classic Regency style, to which the blue-grey local stone is particularly well suited. The stone, which gleams white when wet, has also earned the city the romantic title 'Silver City by the Sea'.

Castlegate is the main square of Aberdeen, and has been so for almost seven hundred years. The earliest buildings survive only in record, but a square tower of the Town House, built in 1622, with a steeple and a spire, still stands as

Union Street, Aberdeen

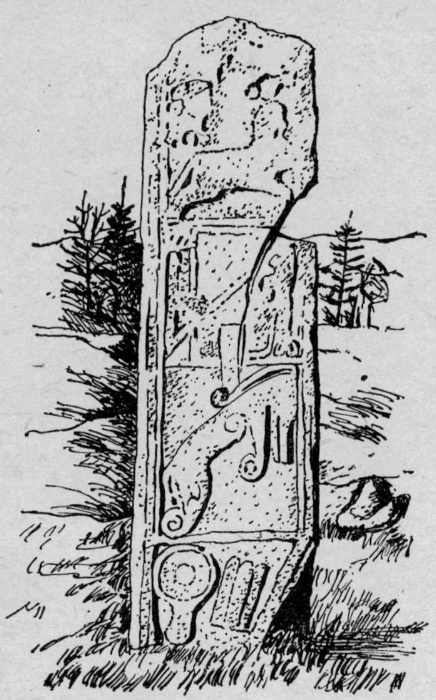

The Maiden Stone, Aberdeenshire

the Old Tolbooth. The most venerable street in the city is the Shiprow. The most impressive building is Provost Skene's House, built about 1545, and later added to.

Aberdeen University was founded by Bishop Elphinstone in 1495. King's College is the oldest part, and the Crown Tower and the Chapel still survive. The chapel choir retains the original oak canopied stalls and the open screens of the French Flamboyant Style. The tower was originally surmounted by a Gothic spire, but this was blown down in the gale of 7 February 1663. Marischal College has been greatly extended, but the original lintel from the old buildings is preserved with the inscription: THEY HAIF SAID QUHAT SAY THEY LAT THAME SAY, the defiant cry of the founder against his critics. King's College and Marischal College were joined in 1860. Since then, many buildings have been added to the University complex.

The cathedral of St Machar dates from the fourteenth century. St Machar was a disciple of St Columba, and originally founded a chapel here, it is said, in AD 580. In 1156 a bishopric was established and a new church built. In 1336 it was destroyed by the English and the Cathedral was rebuilt. The twin sandstone spires of St Machar's Cathedral were added in the sixteenth century. Near the Cathedral is the gorge of the River Don, which is spanned by the 'Auld Brig o' Balgownie', which was possibly built by Robert the Bruce in the fourteenth century and is one of the oldest bridges still in use.

West of Aberdeen, not far from Alford, are two remarkable castles. The older is Kildrummy, which has been called 'the noblest of northern castles'. This thirteenth-century structure has stylistic links with the Château de Courcy, for its curtain wall and round towers are based on the French pattern. Its troubled history is partially reflected in the different styles of architecture which it embodies.

Craigievar Castle, also near Alford, is an L-plan tower house from the seventeenth century complete with turrets and conical roofs, elegantly defensive. It is a fine specimen of imaginative castellated architecture, which was somewhat influenced by the Renaissance.

Evening mood on a Scottish loch ▷

Left: Elgin Cathedral

Below: Balmoral Castle

Fair Isle, one of the Shetland Islands, inhabited by five dozen people

Shetland Pony

In a street of Kirkwall, capital of the Orkney Islands

Scalloway on Mainland, one of the Shetland Islands

The oldest monuments to man's history in the land. Left: a Celtic-Pictish defence tower in the Shetland Islands. Left below and right: burial chamber and fortress, dating from the Bronze Age, in the Orkney Islands

On the following page: the 'Ring of Brodgar', a Bronze Age stone circle in the Orkney Islands

Aberdeenshire is one of the best-endowed counties in Scotland, with buildings of the medieval and Stuart periods. Drum Castle combines both of these elements. Its Tower of Drum is a famous tower-house with battlements 70 feet from the ground and walls 12 feet thick. It is recorded that it was built in the thirteenth century, when stone castles were being built all over Scotland. Adjoining the tower is a mansion erected in 1619 after the Renaissance style. This Jacobean wing has beautiful decorations and portraits in what has been a family home since the fourteenth century.

Almost all of Aberdeenshire's castles are in surroundings of rural beauty, and one might even say that their existence is due in part to the richness of the lands they protected or dominated. But there are traces of even older civilizations than those marked by the castles or ruined monastic settlements such as Deer Abbey on the site of a Celtic church.

The distant archipelagos of Orkney and Shetland retain a character that reflects their history. Orkney was a possession of the Norwegian Crown from the Viking invasion of the ninth century until it became part of Scotland as a dowry in a Danish–Scottish royal marriage in 1468. St Magnus' Cathedral in Kirkwall, the principal town of Orkney, is the only Scottish pre-Reformation cathedral, apart from Glasgow, that has survived intact. Built in the twelfth century, it is of a massive Romanesque design.

Shetland is the most northerly county of Scotland, and Lerwick, its main town, is nearer to Bergen in Norway than it is to Edinburgh, a fact that shows itself in the domestic architecture no less than the street paving. The beauty of the islands, nearly one hundred of them, is rocky, wild and sometimes terrifyingly bare. As the nearest inhabited piece of Great Britain to the North Pole, it has a fascination all its own, especially in the long days of summer when there is virtually no night.